CONTEST WINNERS FOR THREE

Piano Trios from the Alfred, Belwin, and Myklas Libraries

Foreword

Three is not always a crowd when making beautiful music at the piano! *Contest Winners for Three* is a time-tested collection of imaginative trios that can be an exciting part of any piano studio's curriculum, continuing to bring smiles to performers and audiences for years to come.

Alfred, Belwin, and Myklas have produced an extensive list of quality elementary- and intermediate-level piano trios over the years. The pieces included in this volume represent well-loved and effective trios drawn from festival and contest lists, presented in approximate order of difficulty. Divided into five graded collections, outstanding pieces are made available again by Jonathan Aaber, Dennis Alexander, Mary Elizabeth Clark, Margaret Goldston, Joyce Grill, Carrie Kraft, Sharon Lohse Kunitz, Beatrice Miller, Ruth Perdew, and Robert D. Vandall.

Contents

Alfred Music
P.O. Box 10003
Van Nuys, CA 91410-0003
alfred.com

ISBN-10: 0-7390-9927-2
ISBN-13: 978-0-7390-9927-8

Scarborough Fair

Part 3

Traditional
Arr. Carrie Kraft

Moderately

Both hands 1 octave lower than written throughout

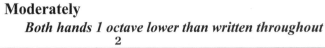

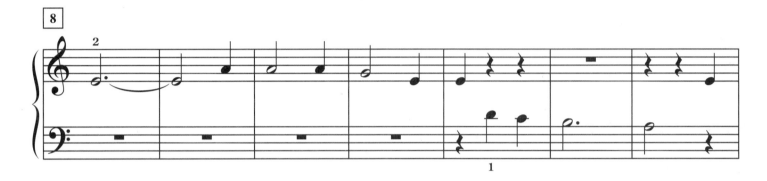

Part 2

Moderately

Both hands 1 octave higher than written throughout

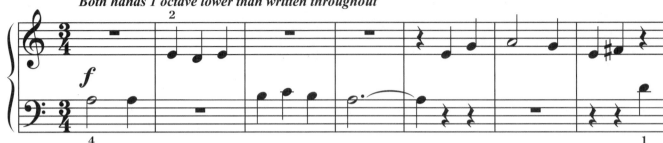

Scarborough Fair

Part 1

Traditional
Arr. Carrie Kraft

Moderately

RH 1 octave higher than written throughout

LH 2 octaves higher than written throughout

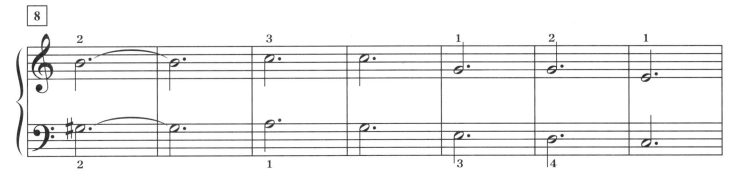

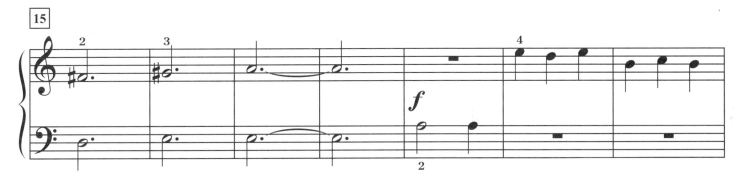

Part 2

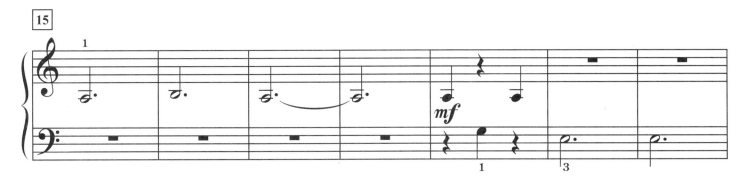

Part 3

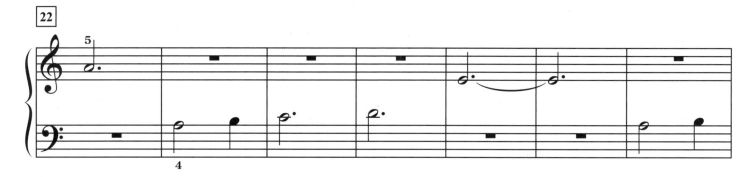

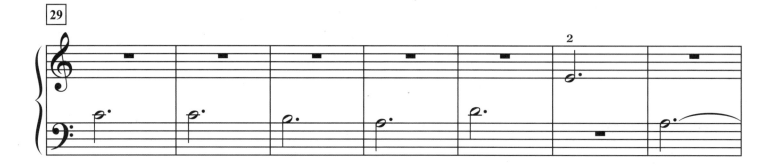

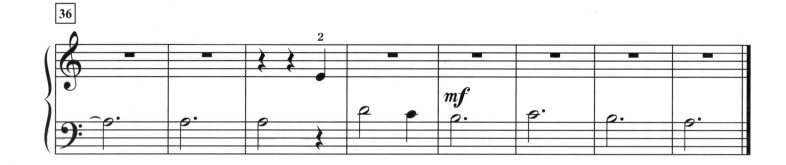

Part 2

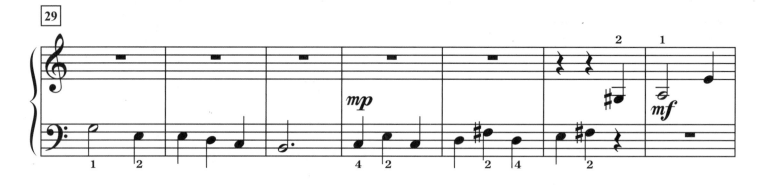

Part 1

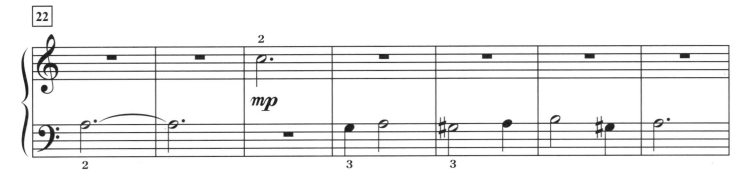

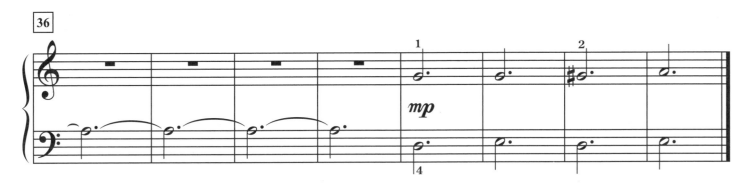

Part 2

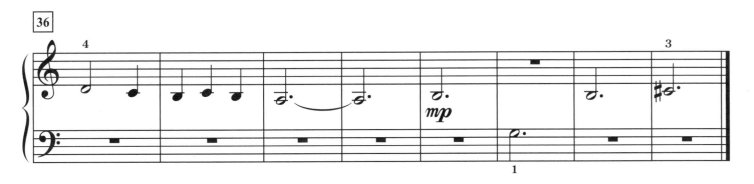

Oh Where, Oh Where

Part 3

Arr. Carrie Kraft

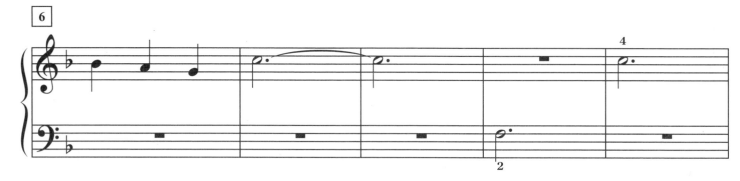

Part 2

Oh Where, Oh Where

Part 1

Arr. Carrie Kraft

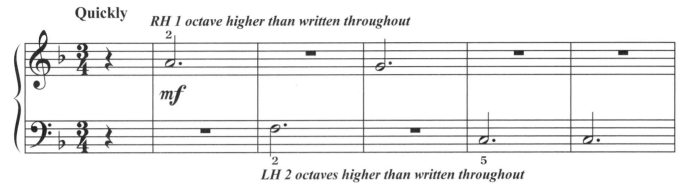

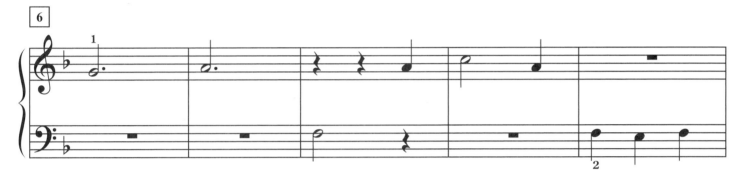

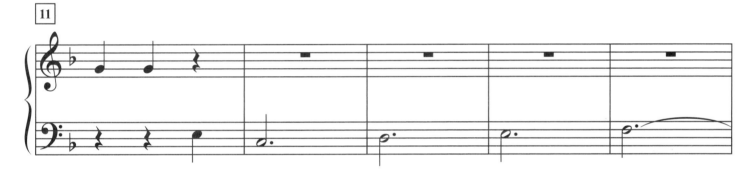

Part 2

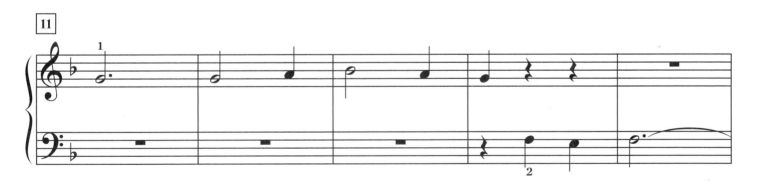

Part 3

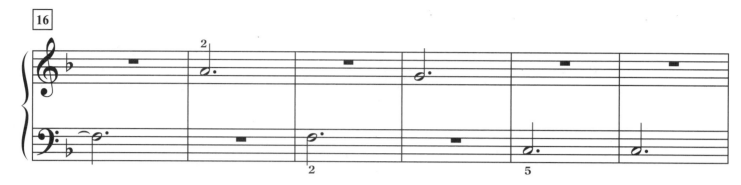

Part 2

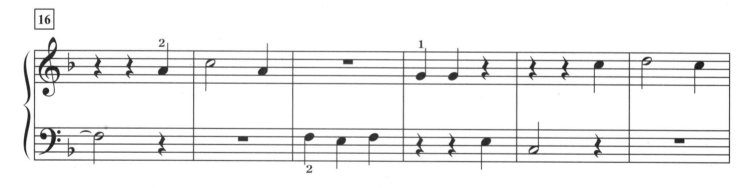

Part 1

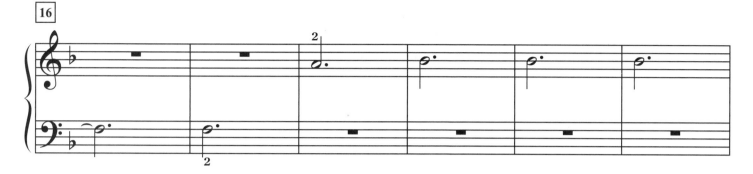

Part 2

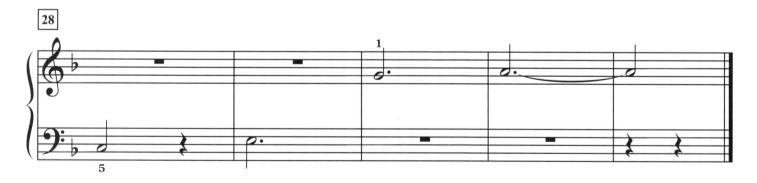

Chopsticks for Three

Part 3

Arr. Eric Steiner

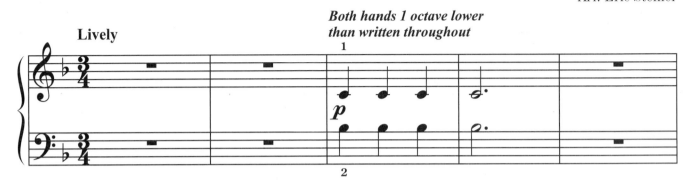

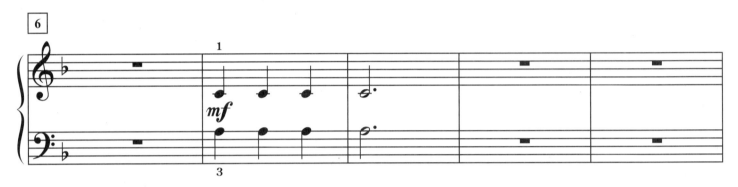

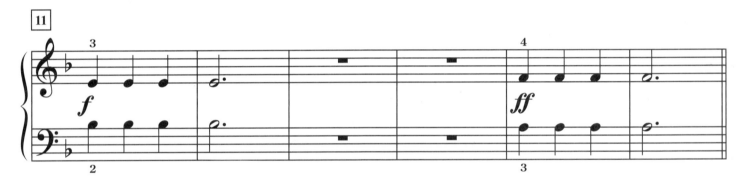

Part 2

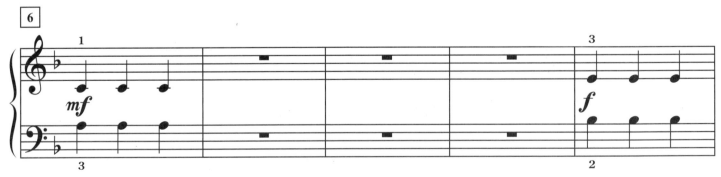

Chopsticks for Three

Part 1

Arr. Eric Steiner

Lively
Both hands 1 octave higher than written throughout

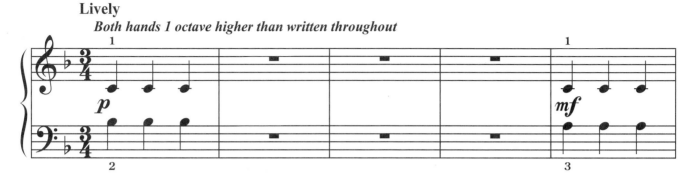

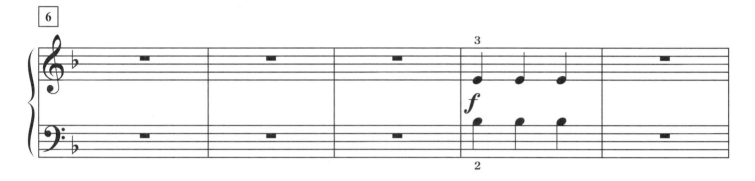

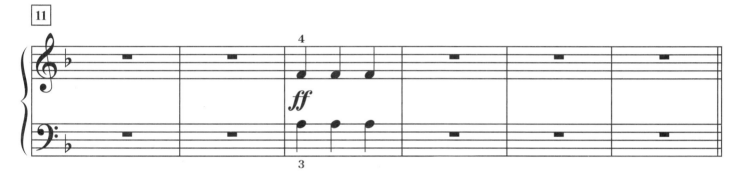

Part 2

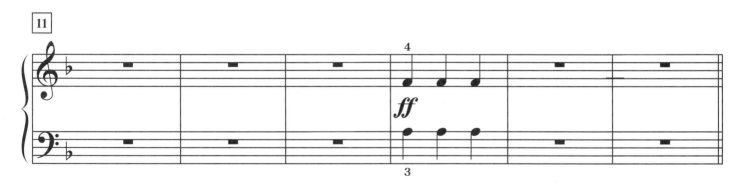

Part 3

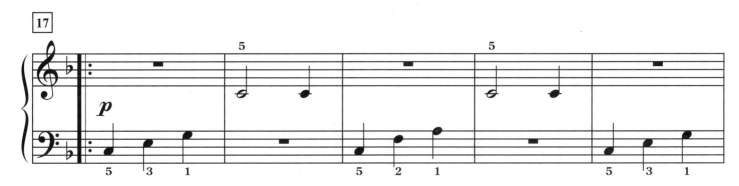

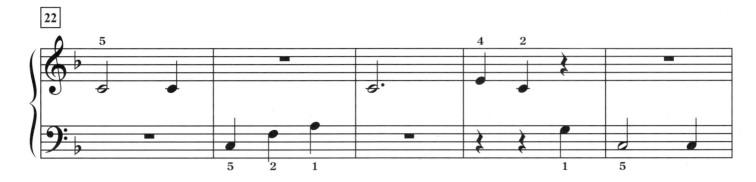

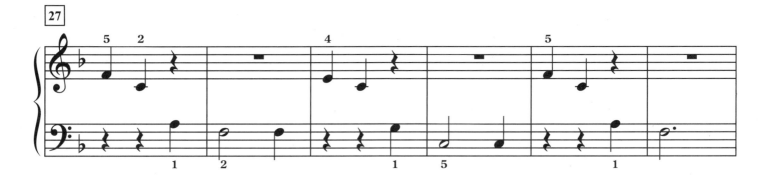

Part 2

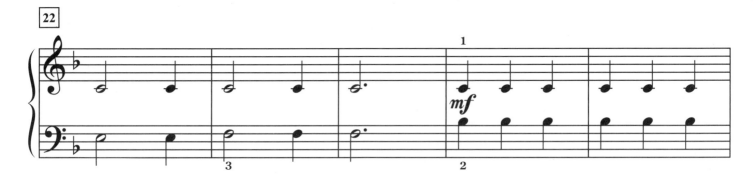

Part 1

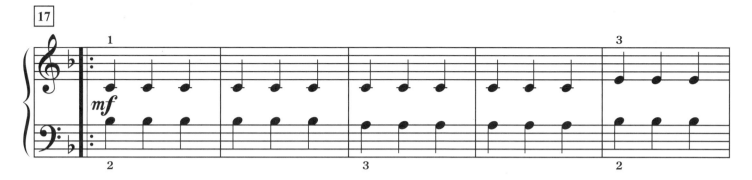

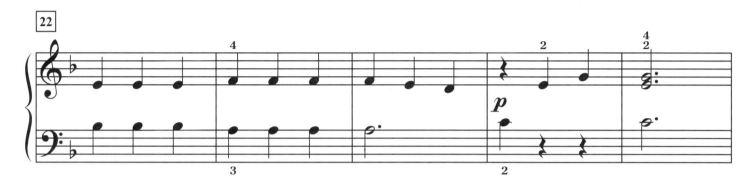

Part 2

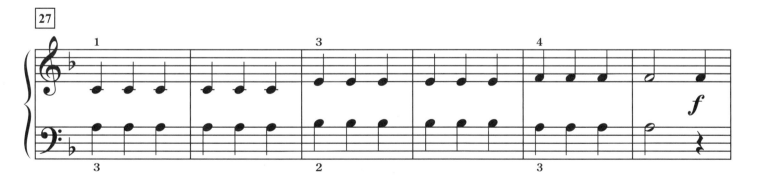

Part 3

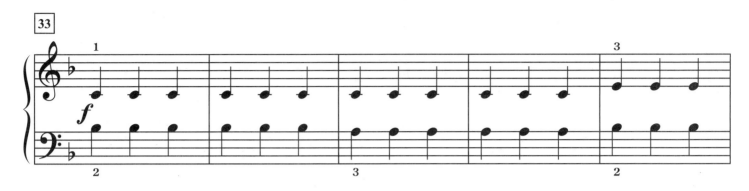

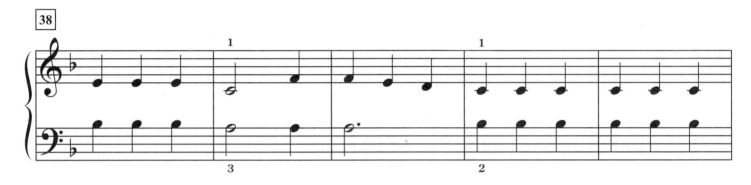

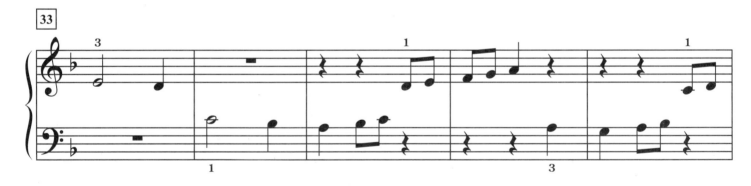

Part 2

Part 1

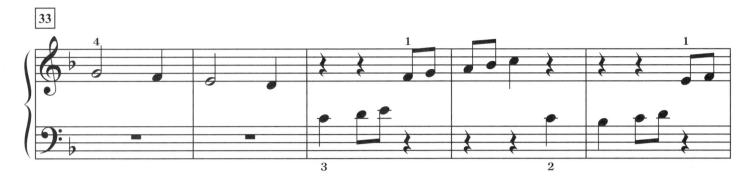

Part 2

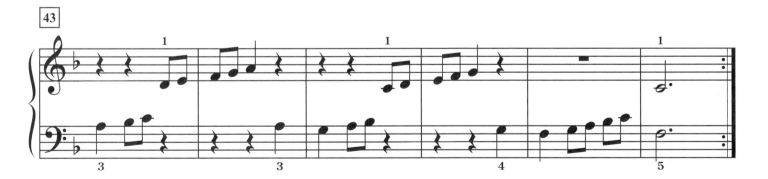

This Old Man

Part 3

Traditional
Arr. Carrie Kraft

Part 2

This Old Man

Traditional
Arr. Carrie Kraft

Part 1

Moderately

RH 1 octave higher than written throughout

LH 2 octaves higher than written throughout

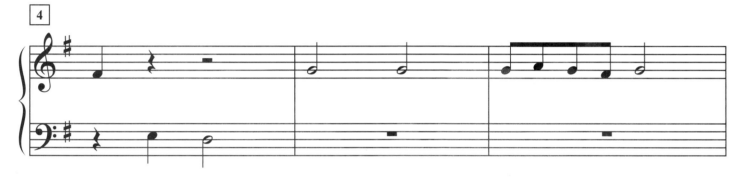

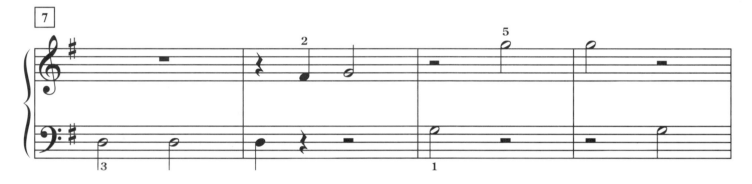

Part 2

LH 1 octave higher than written throughout

Part 3

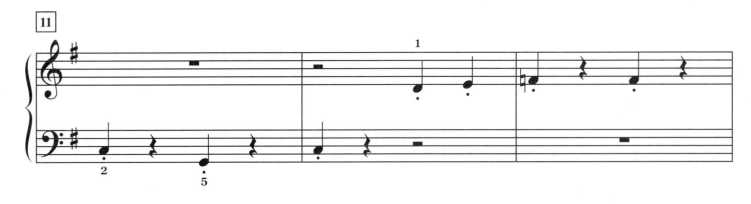

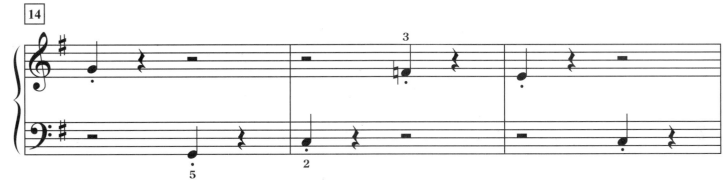

Part 2

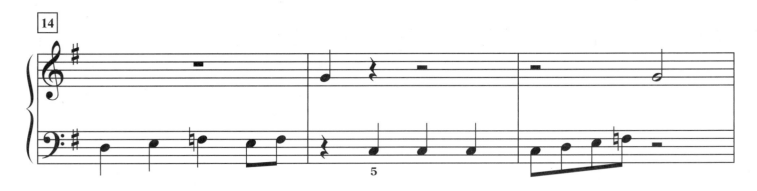

Part 1

Part 2

Part 3

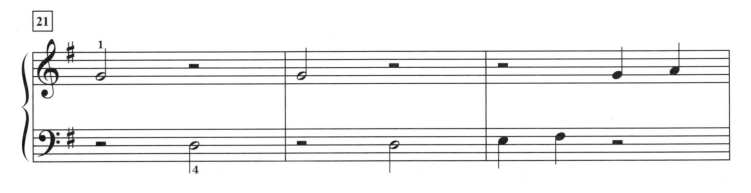

Part 2

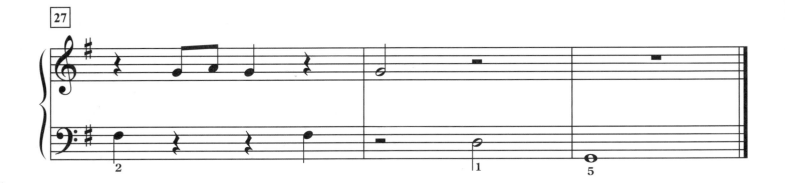

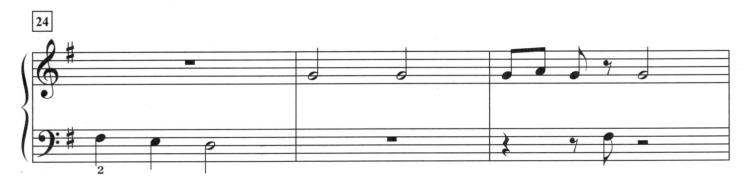

Part 1

Part 2

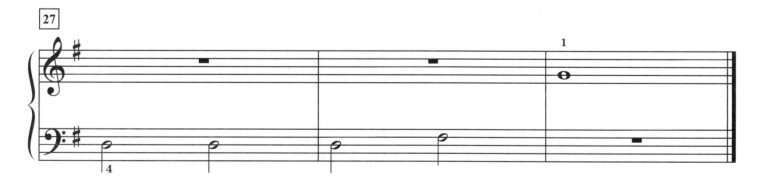

Camptown Races

Part 3

Stephen Foster
Arr. Carrie Kraft

Part 2

Camptown Races

Part 1

Stephen Foster
Arr. Carrie Kraft

Quickly
Both hands 2 octaves higher than written throughout

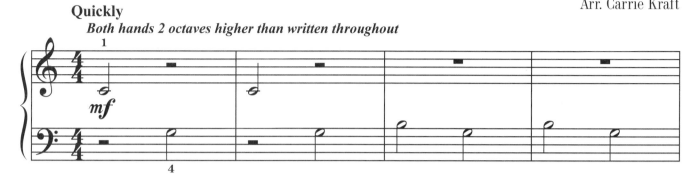

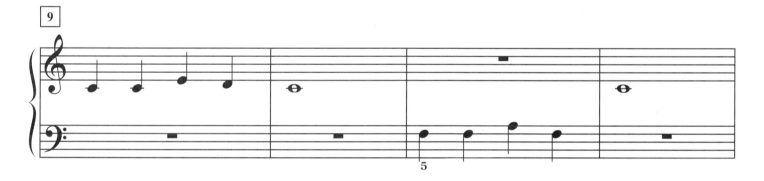

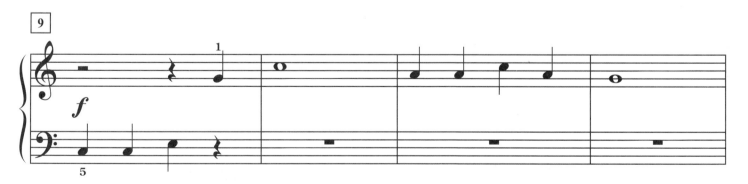

Part 2

Part 3

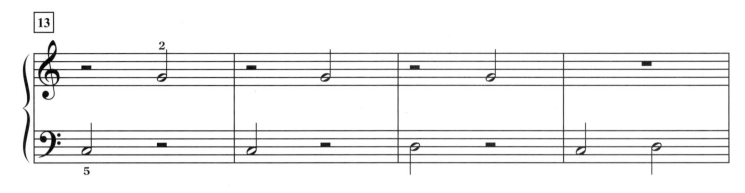

Part 2

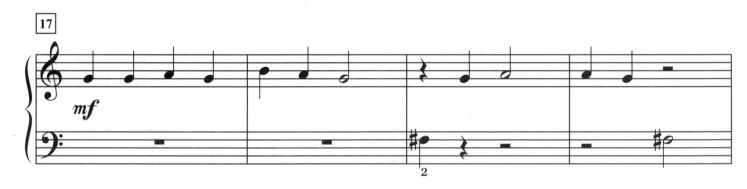

Part 1

Part 2

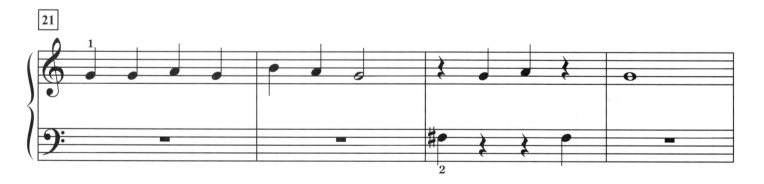

Part 3

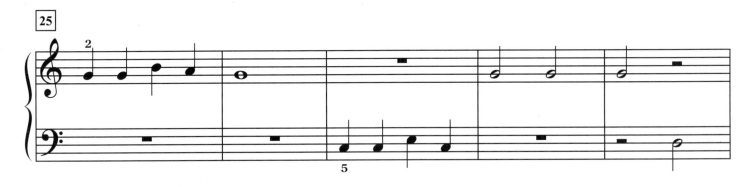

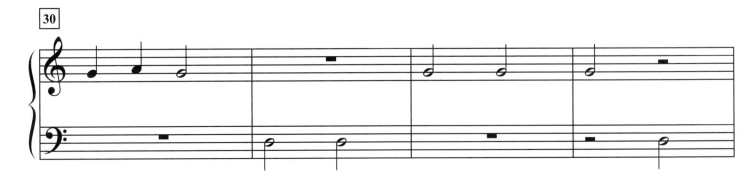

Part 2

Part 1

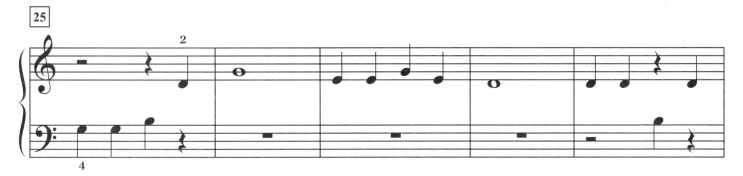

Part 2

Roundabout

Part 3

Traditional rounds
Arr. Mary Elizabeth Clark

Are You Sleeping? (Frère Jacques)

Allegretto
Both hands 1 octave lower than written

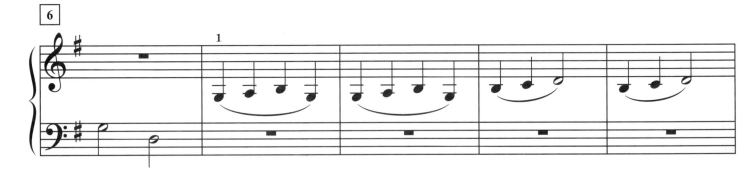

Part 2

Are You Sleeping? (Frère Jacques)

Allegretto   ***Both hands as written***

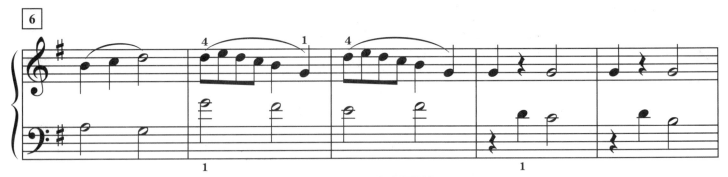

Roundabout

Part 1

Traditional Rounds
Arr. Mary Elizabeth Clark

Are You Sleeping? (Frère Jacques)

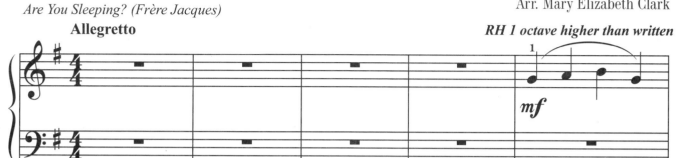

LH 2 octaves higher than written throughout

Part 2

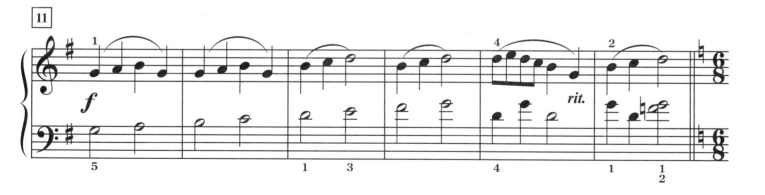

Part 3

17 *Row, Row, Row Your Boat*
a tempo

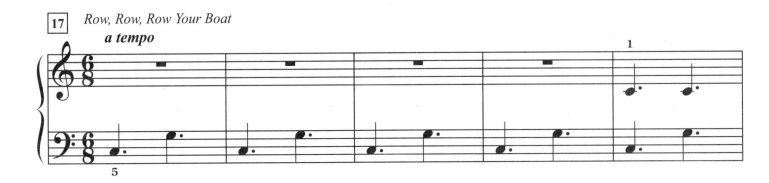

Part 2

17 *Row, Row, Row Your Boat*
a tempo

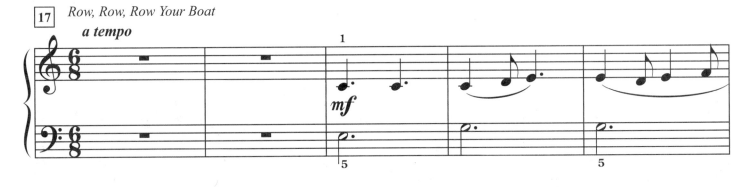

Part 1

Row, Row, Row Your Boat

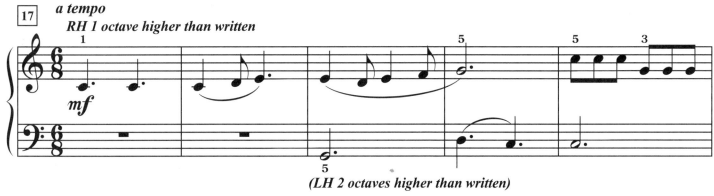

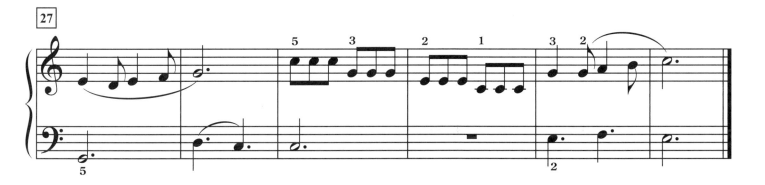

Part 2

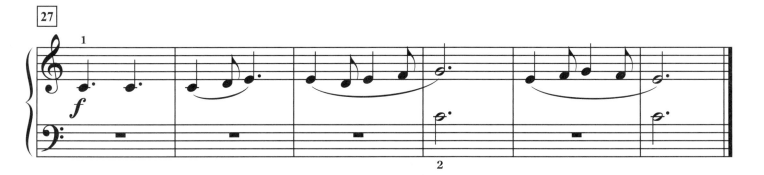